In The Monastery of Fragrance and Panic

Poems by

Miriam Sagan

Contents

in the monastery of fragrance and panic 5

Terminal 7

On a Monument 20

Extended Landfall 21

Neglected Airport Motel 23

The block of marble 24

Diurnal Diary 26

Frontera 32

in the spring twilight 33

a shady path 34

Shadow Puppets 45

Orchid 46

Orange Umbrellas Open In All Directions 48

Light Box 49

Apocalypse In A Little While 51

Accretion 52

The Return 55

in the monastery of fragrance and panic

I sat in the sand of the arroyo

there was no wave to wash my footprints away
other than time
other than wind
other than not knowing
where I was going

I remember when the children
emptied the vegetable crisper
and planted
all the scallions
in the dry wash

expecting harvest?
expecting
cities

these cities, named and nameless,
come and go
with the observer

we could't find
the ruined pueblo
driving back and forth
on arroyo hondo

in the monastery
of tequila and triple sec and ice cubes

I met you, my love,
in bed
and attempted
to lick the salt
off every rim

in the arroyo
of awakening and regret
I crossed my legs
as did the dry bush
as did the reddish cliffs
as did the path
which kept appearing
and disappearing

on a perfectly clear day.

Terminal
in memory of M.B.

0.
before dying
she packs up and ships
her fossils

1.
it was beads on a string, Navajo pearls

it was not like that at all

it was like a tiny Mata Ortiz blackware pot
the size of a thumbnail
no, it was a miniature turret shell
containing
a homeopathic dose
of the sound
of the sea

actually it was more like
a pregnant woman in a great metropolis
weeping at a siren, saying
someone is suffering

2.
someone
asked me if you
had accepted death

this is a problem
of syntax

who is this "you"
does this "you"
exist at all

as to "accept"
I very much doubt it

and when we say death
I'm fairy sure
we have no idea what we're talking about

3.
I know myself
for the ordinary
woman I am
as well as for
the girl
who ran

4.
a man is selling aspen from a truck
next to the Mexican food cart

on my way to see you
I like to go all the way
to the end
of Aurora Street

see the white horse
and the two brown ones
standing nose to nose

curved bird
in the scrub
and panic grass

I just like to go down to the end, turn around
have always been like that

go all the way down
the dead end and wait
for a moment
in the cul-de-sac

5.
what can be covered?

a woman's mouth
lies
treachery
a flame

nakedness
eggs
the dead
our eyes

a table
a bed
arithmetic
the face of the deep

6.
misty coastine
decaying totem poles
in a cubist hand—

you turn the pages
without seeing...

armless torso
of a woman
legless too

sculpted in bronze

7.
I'm alone this morning
sipping a lazy woman's
cup of Nescafe,
I don't trouble myself
that those yellow roses
do as they please

8.
the desert might be
monotheistic
or
homeopathic

you hate it
you love the ocean
Pacific more
than Atlantic

but you are dying here
in town
the neighborhood
slightly run-down

yet a place
someone else
might rejoice in

9.
early maps show it
River of the Mother of God
and then its course
disappears

emptiness—
while the Greek word
for "desert"
transmutes
to "hermit"

I am simply
waiting

I am simply
waiting
to feel

I am simply
waiting to feel
the connection
between your swollen, roped, blue-veined
hands and mine

10.
I believe
there is a prayer
of one word

but what
word
is it

and is it
a word
I know?

11.
black doves among skyscrapers
a sooty rain

better to live here
where nothing ever happens

except for two girls, back neighbors playing their guitars

whose songs
come note by note over the coyote fence

and whose last names
translate, if you choose to
as "black doves"

12.
you fold your nightgown—
actually, I fold it
and place it beneath your pillow
where you can find it again

playing Chinese jump rope—
a chain
you can weave
from rubber bands—

at dusk
on the driveway

fireflies...

oh little sisters of darkness

you knew
even then
I had to go.

On a Monument

o dark angel
come and sit
on my tomb
and fill your stone arms
with fresh flowers

o dark angel
fall through starry eons
to carry an umbrella
and catch a train
to glance at your reflection in a storefront window

o dark angel
fall to my starry tomb
sit and tell me
all about why cemeteries
are next to airports

o dark angel
embrace the beautiful carnations
dyed garish pink and green
I'll listen as you confess
all your loneliness

Extended Landfall

the coast
appears blurry in the rain
like a watercolor
left to run
but this is
land, after a long
voyage by water

so death appears
in old age
the man of ninety
might look
at cherry blossoms
from a gnarled tree
or his own knees
and feel—what
the approach
towards something
that may be familiar
but grows larger

I spent my whole life
looking at another country
in childhood
I imagined pirate ships
and casks of jewels
even now
the hypnagogic aurora borealis
dances before

my closed eyes
on the shores of sleep

it was beauty
I sought
a modest island
with scrub oak
in the sandy soil
gulls
dropping mussels on a rock
a red sail
on a catamaran
and I
looking back

Neglected Airport Motel

mild Thanksgiving Day

television
blares
the president

little volcanoes
out to the west
of Albuquerque

in the Bible drawer
also
a Bhagavad Gita

at breakfast
just me and
some Navajo ladies
heading
        elsewhere

The block of marble

will become a girl—
as girls
we swooned over The Kiss
and how the figures seemed
to emerge from stone
you, however, child
of another generation
child of mine
just said
"I don't like
Rodin"
as if this were
allowable

maybe it's revenge
on the master
who neglected his wife
drove his mistress
mad
who, the poet says,
didn't even really
look at the naked model
instead
his own hands
growing larger
growing older

Venus may be
armless

Winged Victory headless
without a face,
it's raining
in the capital city
at the end of empire
umbrellas in the street
our boots on pavement
tell us
we're not just flesh
no longer captured
by the sculptor's thought
remain unkissed.

Diurnal Diary

Noon:
you always turn back too soon
finally arrive before big rain

1pm:

sculpted boulder might represent desert left behind

2 pm:

look right now!

8 ducklings & their mother
sleeping beneath this bench

3 pm:

yellow bridge over stream that is not my mind
black & turquoise dragonflies dart, or is it flit? away

4 pm

crocheted lace
the word is "tat"
so many
tiny counted minutes
by hand
of hours, happy, sad
faded with age
tattered

5 pm

gravestones
bob and tilt
in a cove of grass
not Victorian
cherubim
but death's head
winged

6 pm

fat groundhog
crosses revolutionary war
battlefield

who left that note
about a stolen trap?

7 pm

clouds massed up
over the sculpture
of a fake porch
as dingy as a real one

I sit on the front steps
think about
knitting

8 pm

things appear temporarily in this landscape

spilled ink
map, topography

or seem permanent
like a glacier

9 pm

fireflies skywriting a luminous sentence in phosphorescence

10 pm

hard rain walking
this isn't Zuni
how could I have forgotten
island of Manhattan
a million umbrellas

11 pm

embroidering
a spiral in silver
the moon
    threads its own needle

midnight

upturned boat   beached dreams

1 am

behind my eyelids
archipelago of light

2 am

what you don't
want
to come
eyeball to eyeball
with

3 am

Indian mound
obscured in trees
an entrance
to the underworld
with all its seduction
of rivers
I turn back from

4 am

hour of the wasp
the spirochete
the rabid opossum
nature's god gone Darwin
and you to fate

5 am

stroked, my father says
you know when you wake up
and can't tell if you're asleep?

6 am

what I'm willing to share and what I'm not

7 am

so glad someone replaced the sponges

8 am

bent ribs of wood
ship or whale carcass

a toad pulsing plump
at the base
of the unfinished
sculpture

9 am

afraid of ticks
and afraid of loss
but it is my great good fortune
to no longer
be afraid of myself

10 am

I know those crows
must be married
by the way she scolds him
even about the weather

11 am

I'd like to make
the gold rim
of the teacup
hum

Frontera

you crossed a border
but left your shoes on the other side

you packed your dental records
and entered the land of the dead

you erased your passport
and tattooed your flesh

you boarded a crystal boat
but glass shatters

you boarded a boat of knots
but weaving unravels

you boarded a boat cast from bronze
but waves froze as amethyst

you changed your name
and went looking for God

in the spring twilight

you turn the violet pages
of a book
of probability

Castor and Pollux
shine
above the hot spring
pool
where you sit
naked on the edge

the Milky Way
appears wrapped
on the coyote fence
like strings of blue lights
left out
since Christmas

the two sides
of a metaphor
aren't evenly weighted
anymore
than the love I feel
for you is

and I've decided
not to appear
on the steps of the poem
after all
I just want
to admire you
from a short distance

a shady path

among rhododendrons
a mansion
built for pleasure
a pool full
of water lilies
a dark lotus
the color of Krishna—
these things
reveal themselves
in a play
of light and shadow
like golden carp
in a murky pond
or like a moment
startled awake
by a red bird

green abstraction
magenta outline
San Francisco Chinatown Windows
small oil painting
hanging
on the gallery's
back wall
and in a flash
I'm there
or, more surprisingly
in a taxicab
out of Keflavik airport
6 am
pouring rain

I lay in the bathtub
at your house
thinking
about the long gone girls
of my so called
youth
until someone opened a door
and I became an old woman

tide going out
moon waxing
both pink and white
beach roses
a man skips stones
a girl
turns away on the beach
as if this were a painting
of a girl
on a beach

huge sculpture
criss crossing beams
frame the hill
red metal
like a Shinto shrine
marking Fujiyama
sculptor
in his wheelchair
watches the crane
lift and bolt
his scaffolding
to the sky

it still surprises me
on a city street
how no one
crashes in to me, and I
avoid their feet—
cinquefoil on the mountaintop
blooms in its crevices
and a yellow throated green warbler
sways on a branch

tide pool, neon green
mermaid hair
one snail—
tiny salt water
Japanese garden

black cormorant, whirlpool
reversing rapids
pulled by tide
Bay of Fundy…
stink of the pulp
and paper plant
a boat
a view from a bridge…
whatever taught me
to see things as they are
not as I wish them:
I'll call "sensei"

in a small box
covered in shells, I crumpled
words I didn't need
any more
"patience" and "remorse"

Pluto
is no longer a planet
but you're still
in my bed
no one knows
how to understand
gravitational
wobble

waiting
for the ferry
to pull
from the shore—
and then
what pleasure!
to be neither here nor there.

Shadow Puppets

West of the sun and east of the moon
beyond the causeway
I strolled this morning without dunes
just boardwalk and green park

through the slatted window blind
across the palm treed alley
a red lantern hung at dawn
by day was just an exit sign

illuminated boxes show
silhouette of a hill
lone pine, classical ruin
minarets, Japan

the sky breaks infrared as rain
each image there is turned again
the mirror shows a passing scene
once more this world spins upside-down

what was I thinking
statue of Shiva was not
no, was, the sea
turning   so enter me

Orchid

homage to Roethke

open-mouthed
speckled adder throat
vulva, promise
of pleasure, betrayal
decadent as Salome
purple on white or yellow dotted mauve
a kiss

real, fake
hanging on palms
by the untroubled pool
in Miami Beach
some touchable regret
about the past
and how dusk
slams down
on the subtropics

and art deco hotels light up
and what can be bought and sold
is beauty
and what can never
be possessed—
the same
flower

the fat poet
goes mad
writes naked
in a room with mirrors
and professors
despise my thesis
which is to believe
the words themselves

I look into the heart
of the petals
as easy to touch
with one finger
the clouded Pleiades
or the great tankers
of the shipping lane
lit up like festive
small cities

orchids might suck
oxygen
from the hospital room
or scuttle away
like the tiny ghost crabs
that live in oysters

or like a pearl—remain
or like the moon—go down
fade out, and bloom again

Orange Umbrellas Open In All Directions

jellyfish blown into the glass paperweight

fake ivy made the mirrored gate more beautiful

a legless man in a motorized chair

a tiny crab in a plate of oysters—its home, our dinner

I bought a pair of jeweled sandals

the wind had anorexia and ate only the swoop of seagulls

purdah's chiffon veil rustled by the sea

untitled, the tracks of the sandpiper might have been in Urdu

I tried to unwrap the moment of my feeling as leaves fell without
season

the tideline deconstructed the Hebrew alphabet

what you meant to say, a white lie, a promise

kissed on the lips, mouth open, by dawn

although I was afraid I was not unhappy

blue anodyne, trembling frond, FOR RENT

Light Box

saguaro, Manhattan canyon, thorn bush
I looked over my shoulder
saw palm trees and the pyramids at Giza

realized I had been nowhere—
adobe house, umbilical cord, grave plot—

and everywhere all at once

trapped behind the wallpaper
in my mother's house
the arabesques and swirls

Victorian figures lining the stairs
in skirts and hats

looking through telescopes (repeated motif)

at some distant gothic crag
outside the suburbs
on the edge of riot, boarded, buildings burned

horizon line obscured
scenes framed and censored

I looked over my shoulder

saw words snipped from the letter
stamps of flowers and birds
cancelled out

realized
I was going

everywhere else

Apocalypse In A Little While

Sitting at the Betsy Hotel
Drinking coffee on South Beach

I've taught myself once again
To say please and thank you

I could weep, pierced by the beauty
Of toast, and palm trees (real and fake)

Surrounded by paintings
Of deadly gossamer jellyfish

Which will inherit
The waste heap we leave the earth

But not just yet, because it is Otis Redding
Singing "Dock of the Bay"

And I write these words
On the hotel chit

For this moment, it's as if
I'll never die.

Accretion

geomancy = science of the
a berm
thrown up by winter storms
full of ghosts—
shrimp
crab
a footprint
filling with salt water
there was the sea
and often
a mild regret
a child's plastic alphabet
tumbled in the sheets
a refusal
a knothole
an expanse
a wish
what small necessary object
you'd lost (in this case a comb)
fingered coral
white as a head of cauliflower
on the writing desk;
the only visible
part of my skeleton
was my teeth
I was wearing my dress inside out
as if trying
to remember something
the aleph

washed by the third wave
the moon
was bigger then
in my childhood
when it first shot
from earth
the power of self-accumulation
blue pool
in a courtyard
bound by darkness
arriving by taxi
at an odd hour
what you dreamed
who you loved
what enormous
currents bore you
unaware
keyless, climbing
the stair—
you beat the tattoo of some as yet
unwritten composition
on my arm
apocalyptic tideline
the ocean
locked and groaning
like a book
with uncut pages
an Atlantis
impossible
to build a sand castle
underwater
a single continuous line creates the pattern
head of a buddha

in red light
on a rooftop
garden
a large starfish
a green bolide meteor
the sense that
the self
was about to be
opened
letters of each word
slipped through our fingers
in the infinite presence
this was desire
this was also
an avoidance
of the personal story
like all landscape

The Return

I no longer live
in a monastery
in the clouds

nor am I any longer
the mother
of a small child

the Southern Rockies
seem pre-disposed
to embrace me

I sit on the swinging chair
just out of reach
of my own
cup of coffee